P9-ARR-952

GUN CONTROL

Essential Viewpoints

GUN

CONTROL

BY KEKLA MAGOON

Content Consultant
Eric W. Mogren, J.D., Ph.D.
Associate Professor, History
Northern Illinois University

ABDO
Publishing Company

CREDITS

Published by ABDO Publishing Company, 4940 Viking Drive, Edina, Minnesota 55435. Copyright © 2008 by Abdo Consulting Group, Inc. Intenational copyrights reserved in all countries. No part of this book may be reproduced in any form without written permission from the publisher. The Essential Library™ is a trademark and logo of ABDO Publishing Company.

Printed in the United States.

Editor: Karen Latchana Kenney
Cover Design: Becky Daum
Interior Design: Lindaanne Donohoe

Library of Congress Cataloging-in-Publication Data
Magoon, Kekla.
  Gun control /
Kekla Magoon.
      p. cm.—(Essential viewpoints)
  Includes bibliographical references and index.
  ISBN 978-1-59928-860-4
  1. Gun control—United States—Juvenile literature. 2. Firearms
ownership—Government policy—United States—Juvenile literature. I. Title.

  HV7436.M34 2008
  363.330973—dc22

                              2007013880

TABLE OF CONTENTS

Dave Bunce, left, and Bruce Schoniger pose at a gun club in Logan, Utah. The two co-founded a northern Utah hunting club.

THE GUN CONTROL DEBATE

*I*t is hard to think about President John F. Kennedy or Dr. Martin Luther King Jr. without remembering that they were killed by assassins' bullets. When tragedies like these happen, people tend to look for someone or something to blame. They are reminded of the destructive potential of guns and they

feel a strong need to make such
violence stop. Some people believe
guns themselves are the problem and
that society should make an effort to
get rid of them. Other people view
guns as things that can be used
responsibly if a person is properly
trained. They believe that guns do

Gun Ownership

As of 1995, there were 220 million firearms owned by private citizens in the United States.

not cause violence, but that people choose to create
violence, regardless of what tools are available.

Guns have been a part of American life for many
years. There is no question that guns can be dangerous,
and deadly. There are 35,000 gun-related deaths in
the United States each year. But guns are also very
popular. Nearly half of American homes contain at
least one gun, many of which are used for hunting and
sport.

The Heart of the Controversy

With so many guns among us, how do citizens stop
them from being used to hurt people? Is preventing
gun violence simply an issue of personal responsibility,
or should communities create rules for public safety?
This is where gun control supporters and gun control
opponents disagree. Some people believe that more

gun control laws are needed to stop gun violence. Others believe that no matter what laws exist, there will always be violence. Still others believe that gun use should not be regulated at all, and that it is a constitutional right to own and operate guns.

Gun Talk

There are many words and phrases used everyday that come from guns and gun culture. Here are a few examples:

Lock, stock and barrel: These are the three main parts of a flintlock, which is an old-fashioned gun. In everyday language, this phrase means "everything."

Ammunition: In gun culture, this refers to bullets. In other instances, the word describes information, resources, or preparation needed to do something, such as to win an argument or complete a task.

Shooting from the hip: When someone carried a pistol in a hip holster, they would have to draw the gun, raise it, and aim before they could shoot. A fast shooter could draw and fire while the gun was still near his hip. Today, this phrase describes an idea or reaction that is given quickly, without much thought or planning.

Half-cocked: Flintlock guns had to be cocked, before they could be used. A half-cocked gun was one that wasn't ready to fire, but could go off unexpectedly if something went wrong. This word now is often used to describe an attitude of sudden, misplaced anger or a rash decision.

GUNS AS A SYMBOL OF LIBERTY

The social and political climate in the United States during the 1980s helped intensify the gun control debate. President Ronald Reagan was elected in 1980, when the country was still in the midst of the Cold War. This is a time when the democratic

United States and the communist Soviet Union were politically opposed. Reagan began a deliberate effort to get Americans thinking about the nature of freedom. He "declared freedom the central value of American life and identified two threats to its survival: communism abroad and big government at home."[1]

President Reagan believed that individuals and state governments should have more power than the federal government. Americans of all different political beliefs embraced this belief and Reagan's redefinition of freedom. His dedication to individual freedom created a political space for the ideas of gun control opponents. The NRA's publicity campaigns and lobbying efforts emphasized the message that a big part of American freedom was the ablility to own guns. As author Eric Foner points out, "For millions of Americans, owning a gun became a prime symbol of liberty."[2]

RETURN TO GUN CONTROL

On March 30, 1981, an assassination attempt was made on Reagan. Reagan suffered a punctured lung and underwent surgery. His staff member, James Brady, suffered major head injuries. The media coverage of the incident caused people to think about gun control laws. The shooter, John

Assassin John Hinckley is wrestled to the ground after shooting President Ronald Reagan.

Hinckley, had used a cheap handgun that he had easily purchased by lying on his gun application.

People did not like the idea that a dangerous person could easily get a gun and use it for such a frightening purpose. The gun control movement took this opportunity to push its message. Sarah

Brady, James Brady's wife, became very involved as a spokesperson for the gun control movement. Her story about the experience of almost losing her husband moved people.

THE BRADY LAW

Following the assassination attempt on Reagan, many people joined Handgun Control Incorporated (HCI) to support the gun control movement. A decade-long fight began within Congress over a piece of gun control legislation that would change the way guns could be purchased and how gun buyers were screened. The resulting gun law was not passed until seven years after the legislation was first introduced.

In 1993, the gun control movement scored a major victory when Congress passed this law, the Brady Handgun Violence Prevention Act, often called simply the Brady Law. The law required gun buyers to submit to a five-day waiting period before taking their gun home. It also instituted a national background check system, requiring each gun purchaser to be verified by state and local law enforcement as an eligible gun owner. Gun control supporters were glad when this law was passed.

Opposing Views on Gun Violence

"The only way to reduce gun violence is to pass laws that give citizens the right to carry firearms. Criminals are less likely to commit violent acts if they believe their victims could be armed."[3]

—Phyllis Schlafly, president of Eagle Forum

"Laws that permit the carrying of concealed handguns do not reduce violent crimes. Criminals might in fact be more likely to shoot potential victims in order to prevent an armed response."[4]

—Authors Daniel Webster and Jens Ludwig

They believed requiring background checks would help prevent guns from falling into the wrong hands. It would not allow people to lie on their gun application forms. The five-day waiting period was designed to prevent "crimes of passion" by giving people time to cool off before taking rash actions.

Lobbying by the NRA

Gun control opponents, particularly the National Rifle Association (NRA), fought the Brady Law at every turn. The NRA is strongly opposed to any legislation that puts restrictions on gun ownership. The NRA tries to protect an individual's right to bear arms. Its large membership has made the organization influential when gun control laws are being debated in the U.S. legislature.

The NRA's gun lobby against the Brady Law succeeded in limiting its scope by including a

*NRA president Charlton Heston holds up a musket at the
129th NRA Annual Meeting & Exhibit on May 20, 2000.*

provision that would phase out the five-day waiting
period after five years. In 1998, the Brady Law's
background check system was replaced by the
National Instant Check System (NICS), which
allows background checks to take place on the same
day that buyers want to purchase a gun.

The Gun Control Debate

The two sides in the gun control debate are constantly trying to influence every piece of gun legislation that arises in the United States.

The main goal of gun control is to prevent violence, but the purpose of gun use is not necessarily to cause harm. In trying to prevent violence, gun control supporters want to create rules that prevent people from using guns so freely. Gun control opponents believe these laws are unfair to good citizens who use guns responsibly. It is important to consider whether violence is the result of guns alone, or if violence is involved with the way people think about guns.

The gun debate touches on issues that are very important to Americans. This society values freedom and individuality, but citizens also want to be sure that their society remains safe. How does one balance these conflicting goals? Where does one draw the line between the right to make personal choices and the government's right to control what people can and cannot do?

*A march and rally are held to protest the NRA
National Convention in Pittsburgh.*

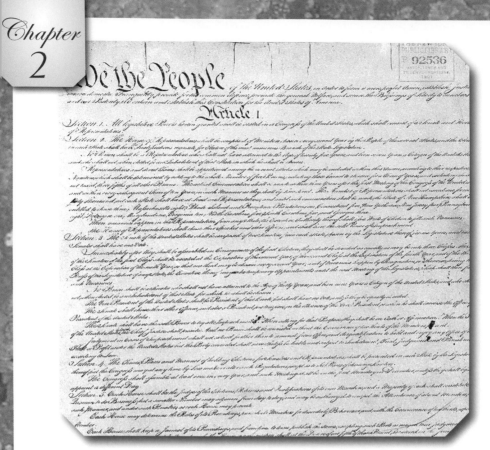

Chapter 2

The Constitution of the United States

THE RIGHT TO BEAR ARMS

The United States Constitution was written in 1787 to outline the laws and beliefs of the newly independent country. The Constitution gives power to the federal (national) government and describes how government can use its power to rule over people.

The founding fathers were also concerned about individual freedom. Amendments were added to the Constitution to ensure that States and citizens would have powers that the federal government could not take away. The first ten amendments are called the Bill of Rights.

As the founding fathers drafted the Constitution and the Bill of Rights, they had heated discussions about how to frame the laws of their new country. It took many drafts to write a Bill of Rights that most delegates were willing to approve. The final language of the Second Amendment reads,

> *A well-organized Militia, being necessary to the security of a free State, the right of the people to keep and bear Arms, shall not be infringed.*[1]

This amendment is the main portion of the Constitution that concerns the gun debate. While it is an important piece of the nation's law, citizens and lawmakers today do not agree on the amendment's meaning. Both sides of the modern gun control debate refer to the Second Amendment as part of their argument in the debate. Why is this amendment controversial, and what circumstances surrounded the drafting of this amendment?

Guns in Early America

When the country was founded, the states had been British colonies. The colonists overthrew British rule in the Revolutionary War, but the new U.S. government did not know if the British would return. When the Constitution and the Bill of Rights were written, the Founding Fathers assured American citizens the right to bear arms for self-defense. This was done to protect citizens in case of an attack on the country.

Not many average people owned guns at the time the Constitution was written. Most Americans who

---

Founding Fathers on the Right to Own Guns

Patrick Henry:
The great objective is that every man be armed....Everyone who is able may have a gun.

George Mason:
To disarm the people [is] the best and most effectual way to enslave them.

Samuel Adams:
The Constitution shall never be construed ... to prevent the people of the United States who are peaceable citizens from keeping their own arms.

Alexander Hamilton:
The best we can hope for concerning the people at large is that they be properly armed.

Richard Henry Lee:
To preserve liberty, it is essential that the whole body of people always possess arms, and be taught alike, especially when young, how to use them.[2]

---

served in the Revolutionary War were unarmed. Approximately 85 percent of the firearms Americans used during the war came from France and the Netherlands. They seized the rest from Great Britain during battles in the war.

Records show that just 14.7 percent of male property owners had guns at the time that the Constitution passed. This figure is fairly accurate, because the government conducted a census of all the guns. They went house to house, asking if the homeowner had a gun, what kind it was, and if they could see it. There were no protests in the legislative records against these gun censuses except to insist that they were not being conducted efficiently enough.

There were not many gun manufacturers in the colonial United States who could make guns. There were gunsmiths, who crafted gun parts and fixed guns, but to earn their living, they primarily made axes, pots, and plows. The U.S. government established Springfield Armory in 1794, which became the first gun manufacturer in the United States.

Gun Ownership: A Second Amendment Right

The Second Amendment focuses on the use of guns for self-defense. When the amendment was

written, self-defense was an important issue
to many Americans. The newly formed country
had no organized national defense system and had
only just fought off the oppressive British rule. At
one point, King George III even ordered that the
American colonists' guns be taken away from them.
In light of this, the Founding Fathers recognized
how important gun ownership was to maintaining
freedom in the newly free country.

In modern society, guns have taken on many
other purposes. The United States now has a
national defense system. Guns are commonly used
by the average citizen for hunting, sport, and
personal protection. These sports and activities are
wildly popular in many parts of the United States.
Approximately 15.1 million Americans hunt for
sport. The gun industry serves many law-abiding
citizens who do not want to see their rights to gun
ownership and use restricted.

When opponents of gun control look at the
Second Amendment, they focus on the portion
that says "the right of the people to keep and bear
arms, shall not be infringed." They understand
the right to bear arms as an inalienable right, one
that cannot be taken away.

Gun Control: Reinterpreting the Second Amendment

The Second Amendment was the first governmental effort to regulate how firearms are used, stating that citizens have a right to own and use guns for self-defense. As the circumstances of life have changed, so have the ways Americans understand the Second Amendment. Advances in gun technology and changes within society have transformed people's fears. Americans are no longer concerned about a British invasion. Today, fears involving guns center on crime, gangs, school violence, and terrorism. While many may share these fears, people take very different approaches to understanding gun use today. Guns can also be used to hurt, frighten, or manipulate other people.

Gun control supporters believe that the Second Amendment must be examined in light of the changing society. They believe the important text of the Second Amendment is, "A well-organized militia being

"The thing one has to appreciate in trying to understand the history of the Second Amendment is that we've had gun regulation as long as there have been guns in America. The Founding Fathers were not opposed to the idea of regulation. In fact, their view of liberty was something that they would have described as "well-regulated liberty." The idea of regulation, the idea of reasonable government regulation, was absolutely essential to the way they understood liberty. In fact, in their view, if you didn't have regulation, you had anarchy."[3]
—*Saul Cornell, Professor at Ohio State University*

necessary to the security of the free State." Gun control supporters think the Second Amendment applies only to militias or organized defense organizations. They do not believe that the amendment applies to civilians.

THE QUESTION OF GUN CONTROL

America is a complex society. Its citizens cannot make individual decisions about gun usage. Lawmakers and law enforcement regulate the actions of a country's citizens and help keep society safe.

Questions that must be considered are: Under the Second Amendment today, is the right to bear arms universal? When the Founding Fathers drafted the Constitution, could they have imagined the power of a machine gun? Does it matter?

Larry Pratt, president of Gun Owners of America, talks at a Second Amendment news conference on March 14, 2006, at the Capitol in Harrisburg, Pennsylvania.

*A flint lock officer's musket produced between 1780 and 1810
and used in the Revolutionary War*

MILITIAS AND SHIFTING
ATTITUDES

*W*hen the Constitution was written, the
United States did not have a
professional army. The state militias served together as
the national military. Each state controlled its own
militia, but none of the states had enough money to

provide guns to every militia member. By guaranteeing "the right of the people to keep and bear Arms" the framers of the Constitution made sure that enough citizens would have guns when militias needed to come together to fight.

It was understood that if colonial citizens were not allowed to keep weapons, they could again be at the mercy of the British army or other invaders. In fact, King George III's order for British soldiers to disarm colonists had been one of the main causes of the Revolutionary War.

Militias were also important for protection within the states. There were no police departments, so militias were the law keepers in some areas of the country. Because the newly created states could not afford to buy enough guns to arm a militia, the citizens had to arm themselves. These citizens then had a responsibility to the state. If there were ever a crisis, they would serve as part of the militia.

After the Revolution

Although the militias fought great battles in the Revolutionary War, some leaders believed that there was a need for a standing army in colonial America.

Early in the war, George Washington told Congress that, "[t]o place any dependence upon Militia, is, assuredly, resting upon a broken staff."[1]

MANAGING THE MILITIAS

Managing the militias was difficult. Militias were made up entirely of volunteers, and most of them were not very skilled at shooting. Early militias were extremely inefficient. Volunteer militias could not be controlled as closely as leaders would have liked. Members often deserted their unit. There was virtually no way to create large fighting units because the members stayed close to home. The militia of one state or area would not necessarily join that of another area. Guns were in short supply, and few people were interested in firearms to begin with.

Because of these problems, the federal government decided to arm the militia. The 1808 Militia Act approved funds to

Early Jails and the Police

Militia members often served as the police department for the towns they lived in. Police departments did not exist at the time the Constitution was written and would not appear in American cities until the Civil War. Sheriffs, assistant sheriffs, and constables existed but were few in numbers. There were not many jails, either.

As punishment for crimes committed, prisoners or people who owed money were sometimes confined to certain sections of the city where they lived. Monetary fines, property forfeiture, and corporal punishment were also common punishments. On some eighteenth century maps, these neighborhoods are sometimes marked. The system was similar to putting people on parole. There were not enough jails and prisons to hold people at the time.

provide guns and military equipment for the combined militia of the United States. Later in the 1800s, the states began forming official militias, which they called the National Guard.

GUN RIGHTS AND MODERN MILITIAS

What is the role of a citizen militia in the United States today? Some people believe that it is still a citizen's responsibility to join the militia in an emergency. Many opponents to gun control do not believe the National Guard is the modern militia. They think non-military citizens should still arm themselves and prepare to contribute to the national defense.

Gun Control opponents argue that the right to defend themselves extends to defending the nation against foreign attackers. In light of recent terrorist attacks, they see this as a very real possibility.

Whites of Their Eyes

Armies fought early American battles on open fields. The famous saying, "don't fire until you can see the whites of their eyes" made sure soldiers could more accurately hit their target. Muskets were only accurate up to 50 yards (45.7 m), which is about the distance from which you can make out someone's eyes.

Gun Control and National Defense

Today, the United States has a professional army that protects national safety and that is made from voluntary citizens. It also has well-established state militias, in the form of the Army National Guard. Some, particularly gun control supporters, believe the National Guard is the modern militia. They see private militias as outdated and unnecessary in light of the current military capabilities of the United States.

In addition, gun control supporters understand "self-defense" as an individual right rather than a collective duty. They do not see national defense as a militia's responsibility.

Increasing Gun Ownership

The earliest American citizens did not have all that much access to, experience with, or interest in guns. However, the relatively small number of guns in the United States began to increase in the mid-1800s. Industrialization created mechanisms for better and faster gun production. It became easier to make and distribute guns, and the cost of purchasing guns went down. As a result, gun ownership increased. New varieties of guns, including handguns, started being manufactured at this time.

Members of the Army National Guard unit based in Elkton, Maryland

Around the same time, Americans underwent a shift in their attitudes toward guns. People began buying guns specifically to use for personal self-defense. This attitude of personal self-defense was very different from the collective self-defense of militias.

EARLY GUN CONTROL EFFORTS

The idea of using guns for purposes other than militia weaponry made people nervous. They began asking Congress and their state and local governments to regulate gun use for the public's protection. Thus, most states began creating gun control laws.

"Show me the man who does not want his gun registered and I will show you a man who should not have a gun."[2]

—Homer Cummings, former U.S. attorney general, 1937

Many states created laws that prevented people from carrying concealed weapons. States conducted regular door-to-door gun counts and kept very complete gun registration records. State officials also banned people from owning guns if it was thought the person would be a danger to society. ⌐

A pro-gun demonstrator holds a sign at a demonstration in Boston on April 24, 2000, in protest of the tough gun laws of Massachusetts.

An 1857 photograph of John Brown, the leader of the historic raid on the federal arsenal and armory at Harpers Ferry, Virginia

GUNS AND GUN CONTROL
IN U.S. HISTORY

J ust before the Civil War, Americans'
concerns about the use of guns for self-
defense changed. Americans knew that guns could be
tools for revolution, as during the Revolutionary War.
Some people began to see that it was still possible for

acts of revolution to occur within the United States. One such act of revolution occurred at a federal weapon's arsenal in Virginia in 1859.

JOHN BROWN'S RAID

Slavery existed in the Southern states until the end of the Civil War. African-American slaves were not allowed to bear arms. A few white abolitionists wanted to use guns to free slaves and to protect free or escaped African Americans from being recaptured. They claimed that the Second Amendment supported the right of citizens to defend themselves against an unfair government.

John Brown was one abolitionist who wanted to help slaves escape and also attack slaveholders. Brown gathered a crew and attempted to raid a government weapons arsenal at Harpers Ferry, Virginia. On October 16, 1859, Brown led a group of men in the attack. Their effort failed and most of the crew died in the attempt.

However, these actions stirred the nation. The idea of individuals and small groups staging revolutionary acts brought the idea of gun control to the forefront. Many Americans began to reconsider the way they viewed the right to bear arms.

THE CIVIL WAR

In April 1861, the Civil War began when South Carolina militia members fired on Union soldiers at Fort Sumter. Southerners believed that the federal government was overstepping its power to create laws for the states, particularly on the issue of slavery. The attack brought to life the Second Amendment's promise to protect the states' right to organize their own militias. It was also the beginning of the

Important Amendments

The Second Amendment is not the only amendment important to the gun control debate.

The First Amendment reads:
Congress shall make no law … abridging the freedom of speech, or of the press; or the right of the people peaceably to assemble, and to petition the government for a redress of grievances.[1]
People can feel free to speak out about their thoughts on gun use and gun control.

The Fourth Amendment reads:
The right of the people to be secure in their persons, houses, papers, and effects, against unreasonable searches and seizures, shall not be violated.[2]
This right protects gun owners from having their guns taken away by the government.

The Fourteenth Amendment reads:
No state shall make or enforce any law which shall abridge the privileges or immunities of citizens of the United States; nor shall any state deprive any person of life, liberty, or property, without due process of law.[3]
Within the gun control debate, this amendment guarantees the ability to own property that citizens can use to defend themselves.

biggest conflict the country had
ever seen. The Union's victory
over the Confederacy restored the
federal government's rule over all
the states.

THE NATIONAL RIFLE ASSOCIATION

The National Rifle Association
(NRA) was founded shortly after
the Civil War, in 1871, as a small
shooting association. Its purpose
was to provide gun safety
education and rifle training to
keep average citizens militia-ready.

U.S. v. Cruikshank

In 1875 the court case
U.S. v. Cruikshank, the
U.S. Supreme Court ruled
that a federal law that
punished individuals for
violating civil rights was
unconstitutional. The law
used the Fourteenth
Amendment as grounds
for federal intervention in
law enforcement. Chief
Justice Morrison Waite de-
livered the ruling. In his
ruling, Waite listed the
right to bear arms as one
right that would have been
protected by the federal
law.

The Department of the Army approved of the
NRA because it helped keep the general population
trained to fight. The NRA worked with the National
Board for the Promotion of Rifle Practice, a group
started by Congress to train the militia. "Public Law
149" passed in 1905 and made it legal for Congress
to sell surplus military weapons to the NRA and gun
clubs. These new weapons helped the NRA grow. By
the start of World War I in 1914, the NRA had
several thousand members.

Gangster John Dillinger near Moore, Indiana, in 1934

At the end of World War I, the NRA received a huge amount of weapons that had been used during the war but were no longer needed. They gave the guns to people in gun clubs. Many soldiers joined after returning home. NRA membership increased to 35,000 members in the 1920s.

RISE OF ORGANIZED CRIME

In 1917, the Eighteenth Amendment prohibited the sale, production, and transportation (including importing and exporting) of alcohol. The period when this law was in effect is called Prohibition.

Many people still wanted access to alcohol, so gangsters and criminals profited by selling alcohol illegally. In the 1930s, the United States experienced the Great Depression. At this time, gangsters were robbing banks and terrorizing communities. Violent shootouts and public battles took place between warring crime groups bearing weapons such as sawed-off shotguns, machine guns, and increasingly effective handguns.

The Eighteenth Amendment

The Eighteenth Amendment reads in part: "the manufacture, sale, or transportation of intoxicating liquors within, the importation thereof into, or the exportation thereof from the United States and all territory subject to the jurisdiction thereof for beverage purposes is hereby prohibited."[4]

LAWMAKERS TURN TO GUN CONTROL

In the light of the rise in violent crime, citizens began to fear how guns could be used. Lawmakers reacted by trying to regulate gun use.

The National Firearms Act of 1934 was the first attempt at national gun control legislation. This law made it more difficult to buy machine guns and sawed-off shotguns, and it outlawed the use of silencers on guns. It also banned other violent weapons, such as bombs.

The Federal Firearms Act of 1938 added additional restrictions on the sale and use of guns but was later repealed by the Gun Control Act of 1968. One of the purposes of the 1938 Act was to start a national system of gun licensing and registration that required participation from gun owners, sellers, manufacturers, and importers.

THE NRA BECOMES A VOICE IN GUN CONTROL

The NRA, while originally formed as a gun club, took great interest in gun control legislation. The NRA was strongly opposed to the Federal Firearms Act of 1938 (and later to the Gun Control Act of 1968). It understood that the purpose of the law was to fight crime, but it believed that gun control laws threatened law-abiding gun owners. The NRA fought against portions of the new laws that affected everyone, such as the proposed system of national gun registration.

The NRA's growing membership and lobbying ability was hard for lawmakers to ignore. With these lobbying efforts, the NRA established itself as a strong voice for gun rights.

World War II and the Cold War

In 1941, the United States entered World War II, and gun production in the country skyrocketed. More guns were available for purchase. The guns were also faster. There were more accurate rifles and handguns, and also high-powered machine guns became available.

After the war, the political climate in the United States changed dramatically. For four years, the nation had focused on defeating Germany and Japan. Now a new enemy had emerged. The United States' system of capitalism and the Soviet Union's system of communism were in conflict, creating an atmosphere of fear called the Cold War.

Many Americans feared communists. They feared the possibility that their neighbors could be their enemies. The right to bear arms became important to many Americans. Citizens wanted to defend the country by protecting themselves, their homes, and their families.

Assassinations

President John F. Kennedy was elected in 1960. He was very popular, although he was elected when the nation was in turmoil. In 1963, President Kennedy was shot and killed by an assassin while riding in a motorcade in Dallas, Texas. President Kennedy's death devastated Americans.

"The only U.S. Supreme Court ruling that actually focused on the Second Amendment, *U.S. v. Miller* (1939), found that there is no individual right to bear arms independent of national self-defense concerns. The Supreme Court has spoken only once, it has spoken in favor of the civilian militia interpretation, and it has not spoken since. If the Court has held a different view, it has certainly had ample opportunity to rule on the matter since then."[5]

— Tom Head, author

During this time, civil rights protests were causing a lot of turmoil in the United States. Civil rights leader Dr. Martin Luther King Jr. spoke out for peaceful protests. In 1968, King was shot and killed while standing on his hotel balcony. That same year, presidential candidate Robert F. Kennedy was killed by a bullet wound after giving a speech. Americans were devastated by the loss of these dynamic leaders.

A portrait of President John F. Kennedy

PROTESTING THE VIETNAM WAR

The United States entered the Vietnam War in the early 1960s. However, during this time, instead of the nation coming together to support the war, a large portion of the country started an anti-war movement. Many young people spoke out against the violence by calling for peace.

Protestors objected to the military draft, claiming that they should have the freedom to choose whether or not to fight. The draft is a government policy that selects and requires men to serve in the military during a time of war. Some protested the Vietnam War by collecting draft cards and burning them or sending them back to the government. These people were opposed to the violence they associated with the right to bear arms. They made an individual choice to not participate in the war rather than following the collective need of the government.

THE GUN CONTROL ACT OF 1968

The Gun Control Act of 1968 added restrictions to the sale and use of guns. The Act banned most interstate gun sales, sales to minors, and sales to people with criminal records. It added legal penalties to crimes committed with a firearm. It also required gun sellers to be licensed and keep records of all gun and ammunition sales.

The Bureau of Alcohol, Tobacco and Firearms (BATF) was created in 1972 and given the responsibility of enforcing the Gun Control Act. The BATF remains the organization with federal control over gun law.

A group of anti-Vietnam War protestors carry boxes of draft cards to a New York City Post Office to send to the U.S. Attorney General on October 16, 1967.

Members of Handgun Control Incorporated protest outside the San Diego Convention Center, site of the Republican National Convention.

KEY PLAYERS IN THE GUN CONTROL DEBATE

uring the 1970s, an organized gun control movement developed in the United States. At the same time, the NRA was growing stronger. Gun rights groups cropped up, as well, to respond to the push for gun control legislation.

In Favor: Handgun Control, Incorporated

In 1974, Mark Borinsky founded the National Council to Control Handguns (NCCH) after being mugged at gunpoint. When he realized that there were no other groups devoted to gun control, Borinsky moved to Washington, D.C., and started the organization. He felt very strongly about ending gun violence and founded NCCH in order to support gun control legislation. Nelson "Pete" Shields, who was the father of a gun victim, and Edward Welles, who was a former CIA agent, joined Borinsky's organization. NCCH was renamed Handgun Control, Incorporated (HCI) in 1980.

In 1980, John Lennon of the rock group The Beatles was shot and killed by an assassin. His murder shocked the nation and deeply upset many of his fans. Thousands of people joined HCI and in 1981 membership grew to 10,000. Borinsky, Shields, and Wells brought HCI to the national stage and soon gathered a following for their work.

In Favor: Coalition to Stop Gun Violence

In 1974, the Board of Church and Society of the Methodist Church created the National Coalition to Ban Handguns (NCBH). This group was comprised of a partnership between 30 organizations who wanted to fight for policies to ban gun ownership. HCI joined NCBH in its early years, but it left the coalition to focus on public safety rather than a ban on gun ownership.

NCHB later changed its name to the Coalition to Stop Gun Violence (CSGV). In 2007, the coalition included 45 member organizations. CSGV continues to push legislation to regulate gun distribution. Its main goal continues to be reducing gun-related deaths and injuries.

"There is a gun crisis in the United States. Between 1933 and 1982, nearly one million Americans were killed by firearms."[3]

— *Violence Policy Center*

In Favor: Brady Center to Prevent Gun Violence

In 1983, The Center to Prevent Handgun Violence (CPHV) was founded as a sister organization to HCI. As an educational outreach organization dedicated to reducing gun violence, it quickly became one of the foremost organizations in the

Former White House Press Secretary Jim Brady and his wife, Sarah, speak to re-porters outside the U.S. Capitol about the expiration of a five-day waiting period for the purchase of a handgun.

gun control debate. The organization sought to raise awareness among the public on gun violence issues and to counter the NRA's lobbying efforts in Congress.

James and Sarah Brady became involved with the organization several years after James Brady was injured in the assassination attempt on President Reagan. The couple dedicated their lives to the organization's work. In 2001, the organization renamed itself the Brady Center to Prevent Gun Violence. HCI was renamed the Brady Campaign to Prevent Gun Violence. The organizations continue to work hand-in-hand. Their mission is to enforce sensible gun laws without a total ban on guns.

In order to gain support, the Brady Campaign tries to share its message with the public. One of the ways the Brady Campaign works to gain support is by gathering information on crimes committed and exposing how those criminals might not have been able to access guns if the laws were different.

Firearms Owners' Protection Act of 1986

Largely due to the NRA's lobbying efforts, Congress passed the Firearms Owners' Protection Act of 1986 (FOPA). It did take some time to pass though. It took seven years after the law's introduction for Congress to approve this law.

This Act once again made it legal to transfer guns over interstate line, removed the requirement that gun sellers must be licensed, and introduced tougher crime laws. The law also made it illegal to use armor-piercing, "cop-killer" bullets as part of the Law Enforcement Officers Protection Act.

FOPA made it tougher for the Bureau of Alcohol, Tobacco and Firearms to conduct inspections of gun dealers, by requiring them to have a search warrant. This Act also prevents the government from making a list of gun owners from the records received from gun dealers.

In Favor: Other Groups

There are many other groups in favor of gun control. The Brady Center to Prevent Gun Violence is closely supported by the Coalition to Stop Gun Violence and the Violence Policy Center. While the Brady Center stands at the forefront, many smaller groups have voiced their support of gun control.

The League of Women Voters, Americans for Gun Safety Foundation, and the Americans for Democratic Action are also strongly in agreement with gun control legislation.

Opposed: National Rifle Association

The National Rifle Association (NRA) was originally founded to train citizens for the militia. The group's founders were Colonel William C. Church, editor of the *Army and Navy Journal*, and Captain George W. Wingate, an officer in the New York National Guard. In its early years, the NRA's membership was just a few thousand people. Its membership increased at the end of World War I and World War II, when soldiers returned home and remained interested in using guns. Thousands of ex-soldiers joined the NRA, and membership increased dramatically.

With such a large number of members, the NRA gained a large amount of political power. Instead of focusing on keeping citizens militia-ready, the NRA now focuses on serving the needs of hunters, sportsmen, and gun owners. They set up gun clubs, rifle training, shooting ranges, and other activities for gun enthusiasts.

As gun control organizations emerged, the NRA began taking a stronger and less moderate position. NRA leaders worried that this new gun control movement could seriously affect the use of guns by private citizens. They began to see the NRA's role as not only to advocate for gun safety, but as national defenders of the individual right to bear arms.

The NRA positioned itself as a national voice for gun rights supporters when gun control became a legislative issue. It moved beyond being a large gun club and began tackling legislative issues. By 1980, the NRA had evolved into a single-issue organization with very extreme positions on gun ownership. The NRA's stand was that any gun regulation was bad, and it put all of its organizing power behind that belief.

To support this position, the NRA shared personal stories about how guns had saved people's lives. However, the NRA's insistence on pushing gun rights

to the extreme has caused it to lose
some supporters. The NRA made
gun control a two-sided issue,
with very little middle ground.
Politicians were forced to take sides
on the gun control issue during
their campaigns. Voters became
concerned about the kinds of gun
laws that elected officials would
support. As of 2007, the NRA had
approximately 4.3 million members. The NRA is
perhaps the strongest voice in the gun control debate.

"The right to defend oneself
from an imminent act of
harm should not only be
clearly defined in [our] law,
but is intuitive to human
nature."[4]

—*Rick Perry,*
Texas Governor

OPPOSED: THE NATIONAL RIFLE ASSOCIATION'S INSTITUTE FOR LEGISLATIVE ACTION

The NRA established its Legislative Affairs Division
in 1934. This division sent its members information
and analyses on prospective gun control legislation.
The NRA mobilized members by sending letters,
writing press releases and editorials, and working with
the media to promote its message. In the 1930s, there
were no groups fighting for gun control legislation.
The NRA's lobbying was unchallenged for many years.
It was successful in limiting some of the provisions set
out in the National Firearms Act of 1934 and the

Federal Firearms Act of 1938. It also helped to shape the terms of the Gun Control Act of 1968.

The Legislative Affairs Division expanded and in 1975 became known as the Institute for Legislative Action (ILA). As lawmakers were considering more and more gun control laws, the institute responded by rallying NRA members to protest the suggested limitations on gun ownership. The institute has developed good systems for getting their members to show support or opposition for different pieces of gun legislation that are introduced.

Opposed: Other Groups

There are many other groups that oppose gun control legislation. While small and large organizations alike take an interest in gun control, the NRA/ILA remains the dominant voice in the opposition.

Other groups include the Second Amendment Foundation, Gun Owners of America, and the Citizens Committee for the Right to Keep and Bear Arms.

National Rifle Association president Charlton Heston blows a kiss to a supporter during a political rally in Springdale, Arkansas, on October 31, 2002.

George Romanoff, owner of a sporting goods store in Pennsylvania, shows a handgun to John Cypher.

Arguments in Favor of Gun Control

un control supporters believe that the Second Amendment not only supports gun control but also requires it. They point to the first half of the amendment, "A well-regulated Militia, being necessary to the security of a free State."[1] Gun control supporters claim that this means gun ownership must be restricted to militia members, or at least that gun ownership must be well regulated. "The people" that the Second Amendment refers to, they say, are citizens as a collective part of society.

> **Second Amendment in the Supreme Court**
>
> The Supreme Court has never struck down a gun control law on Second Amendment grounds.

In addition to debating the Second Amendment, gun control supporters focus on specific issues regarding the gun control debate. They are concerned with everything from the purchase of guns to public safety. They try to inform the public about their findings and also influence legislation.

In Favor: Getting Guns Is too Easy

According to John Horowitz, Executive Director of the Coalition to Stop Gun Violence, about 60 percent of guns are bought through licensed dealers. The rest are bought at gun shows, through person-to-person sales, and on the Internet. Gun dealers are required to be licensed to sell firearms, though the laws about licensing vary by state. In some states, gun dealers must be licensed before they can sell any kind of gun.

Plastic Guns

The Undetectable Firearms Act of 1988 made it illegal to make, import, or sell plastic guns. Plastic guns are undetectable in walk-through metal detectors and x-ray machines, which are commonly used in airports.

In other states, gun dealers must be licensed to sell handguns but they can sell rifles and shotguns without being licensed. Places that sell guns include gun specialty stores, pawn shops, hunting specialty stores, some sporting goods stores, and some mass-market retailers such as K-Mart and Wal-Mart.

Gun control supporters worry about person-to-person sales and gun show sales, which take place outside of the regulations of gun stores. Individual gun owners often sell their guns without conducting background checks on the buyers. This means that people who could not buy a gun from a licensed dealer, such as convicted felons, mentally ill people, and people under age 18, could potentially buy a gun from someone else. These sales can also take place without any waiting period or purchase limits.

In Favor: Concealed Weapons Are a Danger to Public Safety

In order for individuals to carry handguns in public, they must obtain a license to carry a concealed weapon.

Ohio Attorney General Jim Petro answers questions on April 1, 2004, during a news conference on Ohio's Concealed Carry Law at his office in Columbus, Ohio.

A few states require gun purchasers to obtain a license prior to buying any handgun, whether or not they want a concealed weapon license as well.

Gun control supporters believe the fewer guns allowed on the street, the better. They argue that most people with concealed carry licenses are not trained to use their weapons safely, so their possession of guns puts the general population at risk, rather than keeping them safe.

In Favor: Guns in the Home Should be Stored Safely

People who keep guns in the home choose a variety of means for storing their weapons. Some people choose to keep them unloaded and locked away, while others choose to keep loaded guns readily on hand. Gun control supporters hope to see laws that will require safe storage of guns, but not many currently exist. Without such laws, guns may be kept loaded, unlocked, and accessible to people who should not have access to them, such as children and mentally ill family members. Guns in the home are more often used against family members than intruders or criminals.

Child access prevention laws in 18 states hold adults responsible if they kept a firearm in a place where the child was able to access and use it without permission. The age of the child covered by the law varies by state, as does the penalty for violating the law. A few of these states also penalize adults for keeping a firearm in an accessible place, whether or not a child finds the gun.

In Favor: Gun Ownership Correlates to Increased Gun-Related Deaths

Handguns have become especially popular with the increase in gun ownership. As handgun purchases increase, so do the rates of gun death. Suicide is five times more likely to happen in homes with guns than homes without guns. Gun control lobbyists say these deaths can occur in homes and can be suicides or murders within friendships, families, or relationships. Gun control supporters are bothered by this connection.

Supporters of gun control feel that guns are a threat to public safety. Groups like The Brady Center regularly publish research studies that show how dangerous gun ownership can be.

In Favor: Background Checks Need Improvement

Federal law requires background checks to be performed on people purchasing handguns. These background checks screen gun purchasers for criminal records as well as a history of mental illness, though only 17 states submit their residents' mental health information to the background check system.

Eighteen states require some form of waiting period between the time a person decides to buy a gun and the

Violent Crimes

Guns are used in about 800,000 violent crimes each year.

time the person can take the gun home. Some of these states require that the gun buyer have a permit which have various waiting periods. Waiting period laws are designed to inhibit "crimes of passion" by giving angry and upset people time to cool off before pursuing action with a gun.

Still, gun control supporters do not feel these laws are sufficient. Since background checks have become required by law, there have been hundreds of prosecutions of gun sellers who have violated the law. There is no telling how many ineligible individuals have purchased guns during that time. ⟶

Yvette Tucker Griffin, left, and Carolyn Peters, who lost their sons in shootings, cry during the second "Million Mom March" at the Capitol in Washington, D.C., on May 9, 2004.

Pro-gun demonstrators outside the Statehouse in Boston on April 24, 2000

ARGUMENTS AGAINST GUN CONTROL

The NRA and gun supporters argue that gun control laws are unconstitutional. They point to the second half of the Second Amendment, "the right of the people to keep and bear arms, shall not be infringed,"[1] and claim that it protects each person's right to bear arms without limitation. "The people" that the Second Amendment refers to, they say, are citizens as individuals.

OPPOSED: WIDESPREAD GUN OWNERSHIP WOULD DECREASE GUN-RELATED DEATH

The NRA challenges the correlation between gun ownership and gun-related death. They believe that if more people had guns for self-defense, these kinds of crimes would not happen as often. The NRA argues that it does not matter what kind of gun control laws are in place, because most of the acts that gun control laws try to prevent are already illegal.

Gun control opponents believe people should not treat accidental gun deaths any differently than another accident. The possibility of a car accident does not stop people from owning and driving cars, so it should not be any different for owning a gun.

OPPOSED: BACKGROUND CHECKS DO NOT WORK

A 2007 Gallup poll found that more than 53 percent of Americans believe that current gun laws need to be better enforced before the government begins enacting new ones. Gun control opponents believe that background checks are ineffective.

Opponents to gun control suggest that the government is not enforcing the current laws to their full extent. Wayne Lapierre, NRA Executive Vice President, has suggested that the Brady law background check system is failing because people who do not pass the check are not being punished for trying to get a gun.

In addition, gun control opponents feel background checks are unfair to law-abiding citizens. Because they understand gun ownership to be a Second Amendment right, they do not feel they must submit to background checks and waiting periods.

Mail Order Guns

In 1965, Congress considered passing a bill that would regulate the purchase of guns through the mail. This bill was prompted in part by the fact that Lee Harvey Oswald, President Kennedy's assassin, had ordered his gun through the mail. In fact, he purchased his gun from an advertisement in one of the NRA's publications, *American Rifleman*.

The NRA did not want its reputation damaged and did not want to see rights taken away from gun owners because of Oswald's actions. They sent out letters, press releases, and other messages asking their wide membership base to help them lobby against the proposed bill. It worked. NRA members sent 12,000 letters to the White House and over 3,000 letters to Congress asking their representatives to vote against the bill.

The lawmakers could not ignore this outpouring of feedback from the citizens. The bill did not pass.

Opposed: Gun Control Discriminates Against African Americans

Historically, race has had an important role in gun ownership laws. During slavery, African Americans were not allowed to own or use guns. Slave owners were afraid of slave revolts and wanted to keep African Americans in an inferior and powerless position. The Fourteenth Amendment gives African Americans the same rights as whites to own arms and to act in self-defense.

Many African Americans believed that gun control policies were historically designed to discriminate against them. Laws eliminating cheap handguns prevented poor people from purchasing guns for self-defense, and many African Americans were poor. Some felt that the laws within cities that prevented the concealed carry of handguns unfairly targeted African Americans during the 1960s, as most African Americans then lived in urban areas. Rural communities were more likely to allow the concealed carrying of handguns.

African Americans had been oppressed for many years under the laws of slavery and segregation. They embraced the idea of owning guns for self-defense, perhaps as a result of feeling powerless for so many years.

Opposed: Concealed Weapons Offer People Protection

Different states have different laws about who is eligible for concealed carry licenses and have specific rules for the use of those weapons. Some states allow anyone who is eligible to own a handgun to receive a concealed carry permit. Other states restrict concealed carry licenses to law enforcement officers, private detectives, and others with training and a specific need for a concealed weapon. This can be confusing to gun owners.

Gun control opponents support an individual's right to carry a concealed weapon. They believe that law-abiding citizens with concealed weapons can help prevent crime and respond with deadly force if necessary in a threatening situation.

"Prices as low as $8 or $10 have placed concealable handguns within reach of multitudes who never before could afford them.... [We support barring] these miserably-made, potentially defective arms that contribute so much to rising violence."[3]

—NRA editorial, 1968

Opposed: Guns Can Be Purchased Illegally by Criminals

There are many ways that people buy guns illegally. Most of the guns purchased illegally in the United States were created by legitimate gun

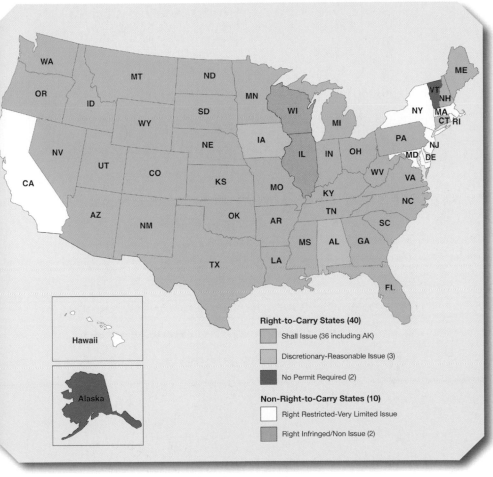

Gun laws by state, as of 2006

Right-to-Carry States (40)

Shall Issue (36 including AK)

Discretionary-Reasonable Issue (3)

No Permit Required (2)

Non-Right-to-Carry States (10)

Right Restricted-Very Limited Issue

Right Infringed/Non Issue (2)

manufacturers and then sold to licensed gun dealers. Some of those gun dealers then turn around and, knowingly or not, sell the guns to people who use or resell them illegally. Guns are also often stolen in bulk from licensed gun dealers who may not have adequate security practices to protect the guns in their possession.

Illegal purchases are regularly made at gun shows, where legal loopholes allow unlicensed buyers and sellers to meet. Individuals nationwide can fairly easily locate and purchase guns drifting in illegal markets on the "street."

Gun control opponents point to this illegal activity. They say that criminals have no problem finding illegal guns to purchase. Therefore, laws restricting legal purchases do not help prevent crime.

"I come from a state where half the folks have hunting and fishing licenses. I can still remember the first day when I was a little boy out in the country putting a can on top of a fencepost and shooting a .22 at it. I can still remember the first time I pulled a trigger on a .410 shotgun because I was too little to hold a .12 gauge. ... This is part of the culture of a big part of America. ... I live in a place where we still close schools and plants on the first day of deer season, nobody is going to show up anyway. ... We have taken this important part of the life of millions of Americans and turned it into an instrument of maintaining madness. It is crazy."[4]

—President Bill Clinton, comments at the Brady amendment signing in 1993

A gun retailer tends to his booth while surrounded by shotguns and rifles at the Western Americana Gun Show in Pomona, California, on February 19, 2000.

Injured occupants are carried out of Norris Hall at Virginia Tech on April 16, 2007, after shootings resulted in multiple deaths and injuries.

GUNS AND MINORS

The majority of Americans are eligible to legally purchase and own firearms. Gun purchasers have to be adults over age 21, must show valid identification, and must not be a convicted felon. In addition, federal law prohibits people who have been legally determined to have mental illnesses or mental deficiencies from purchasing guns, as well as people who have been involuntarily institutionalized for mental health reasons. Seventeen states require people to secure special permits or safety certificates before purchasing handguns. A few states require permits for owning hunting rifles and shotguns.

Though federal law requires gun buyers to be over age 21, juvenile possession laws only cover youth up to age 18. This gap in the laws means that people under age 21 but over age 18 can legally purchase guns in most states, though not from federally licensed gun dealers. Eighteen states prohibit or regulate sales to people under age 21. The rest place no limits on such sales. People in that age range can generally buy guns person-to-person or through other secondary means of sales.

Survey Says

A 2003 nationwide survey about teenage attitudes toward guns found that:

• 39 percent said they know someone who has been shot

• 37 percent said they could get a handgun "if I really wanted to"

• 27 percent know of a handgun kept in their house, apartment, or car

• 59 percent do not believe that "video games can make teenagers violent"

• 56 percent do not want armed security guards patrolling their schools

• 90 percent do not believe that teachers and principals should be able to "bring handguns to school to protect students"[1]

— *Teenage Research Unlimited, June, 2003*

STOCKTON, CALIFORNIA

President George H. W. Bush was elected in 1988. He was a member of the NRA and a pro-gun politician. Bush spoke during his campaign about his belief in the constitutional right to bear arms. It was anticipated that President Bush would support the NRA's position in the gun debate.

A 1989 schoolyard shooting in Stockton, California, changed President Bush's feelings about the individual's right to bear arms. A man shot and killed five children and wounded 30 others.

Tragedy in Blacksburg

On April 16, 2007, a Virginia Tech student with a history of mental illness took two handguns into a classroom building and killed 30 people and then killed himself. Earlier that morning, he shot and killed two other students in a dorm room. At least 15 additional people were injured in the attacks. It was the deadliest single-incident shooting in the country in recent history.

This tragic incident reignited debate about gun control in America. The killer was able to purchase his guns legally under Virginia law, despite his history of depression and mental illness. The state performed the instant background check, rather than a more detailed law enforcement check. Under Virginia law, gun buyers are restricted to purchasing one gun per month. The student purchased one gun a month prior to the shootings, and a second just days beforehand. Gun control supporters point to these laws as flawed because they allowed a troubled individual to buy a gun instantly, easily, and legally.

Gun control opponents argue that the Virginia Tech security procedures and the school's prohibition of guns on campus are to blame. They believe that gun laws would not have prevented an individual from acquiring guns. They argue that if guns had been allowed on campus, students in the classrooms would have been able to defend themselves.

He used an AK-47 assault rifle that had been imported from China. After the tragic shooting, President Bush immediately ordered a ban on AK-47s and other assault rifles. President Bush began to reconsider some of the gun control laws that he had opposed.

Other School Shootings

Unfortunately, the Stockton, California, school shooting was not a singular incident. Dozens of school shootings have occurred across the country.

In March 1998, two middle school students killed four classmates and a teacher in Jonesboro, Arkansas. In 1999, two teenage boys brought assault weapons into Columbine High School in Littleton, Colorado, where they shot and killed 15 people and wounded others. In 2006, a man entered an Amish School house in Georgetown, Pennsylvania, and killed six young girls in their classroom. In 2007, a Virginia Tech university student shot and killed 32 people in a rampage on campus.

Number of Guns in America

In 1790, there were enough guns in the United States to arm 45 percent of all those enlisted in the militia, which was 20 percent of the adult white males and 4.5 percent of the nation's total population. That compares today with an estimate that there are enough guns in America to arm about 120 percent of the population.

Minors and Guns: A Call for Gun Control

School shooting tragedies have raised concerns for gun control supporters. They began to push for laws that would prevent troubled people from gaining access to guns. After the Columbine High School massacre, the gun control movement fought for new legal measures to restrict access to certain kinds of guns. The measure narrowly passed in the Senate with a one-vote margin.

U.S. Firearm Industry

From 1977 to 1996, the U.S. firearm industry produced:

- 85,644,715 firearms
- 39,024,786 handguns
- 26,651,062 rifles
- 19,969,867 shotguns

Gun control supporters argue in favor of preventing youth access to guns, limiting gun violence on TV, and changing youth perceptions by removing guns from homes. A related movement acted to limit the violence that young people see on television, in movies, and in video games. Through rating systems and parental controls, some of those concerns have been addressed. The primary message gun control supporters voice, though, is not what motivates young people to commit violent acts, but rather how to limit their access to violent tools.

A participant holds up a sign reading "Stop the Madness" during a memorial service for the victims of the shooting rampage at Columbine High School.

Minors and Guns: Teach Responsibility

The NRA argues that additional gun control laws would never really work because most acts that gun control laws try to prevent are already illegal. Bringing any gun to school is illegal. It is also illegal for minors to have access to certain kinds of guns. And of course, shooting or shooting at another person is illegal. Gun supporters say that new gun laws would do little to prevent illegal acts.

Guns and Respect for Life

During his 2000 presidential campaign, President George W. Bush commented that gun crime is less an issue that can be solved through legislation and more a "matter of culture—a culture that somewhere along the line we've begun to disrespect life."[2]

Actor Charlton Heston, as the spokesman for the NRA, has spoken repeatedly about the NRA's position on youth recruitment as a tool of gun violence prevention. The NRA seeks to instill in young people a respect for the power of guns by teaching them how to use guns appropriately. It seeks to continue the American gun culture, with its tradition of hunting, sportsmanship, and the right to bear arms for self-defense.

Bruce Musetti, right, holds a rifle up for his nephews while attending the National Rifle Association's (NRA's) annual meeting and exhibition at the Orange County Convention Center on April 26, 2003, in Orlando, Florida.

Senate Minority Leader Tom Daschle and Patty Nielson, a teacher at Columbine High School, appear at a forum aimed at promoting passage of gun control legislation on May 15, 2000.

RECENT DEVELOPMENTS IN GUN LEGISLATION

un control is an issue that ultimately must be decided by legislators. Both sides of the debate try to influence lawmakers so that laws reflect their views. Although gun control has taken a backseat to other legislative issues, there have been important developments on the issue in recent years.

Early 1990s Gun Control Legislation

The Crime Control Act of 1990 primarily created Drug-Free School Zones. This law made it illegal to posess or discharge guns on school property or within 1,000 feet (304 m) of a school.

The Violent Crime Control and Law Enforcement Act passed in September 1994. Its chief feature was the Federal Assault Weapons Ban, which prevented the manufacture and sale of semiautomatic weapons. The ban listed 19 types of guns, and included a list of the features of an assault weapon that were prohibited for any new weapons. The act also included the Violence Against Women Act, increased the scope of the death penalty for certain offenses, and several other components dealing with law enforcement, gun ownership, and gang participation.

Firearm Deaths

In the United States in 2003:

- 730 people died due to accidental firearms discharge.
- 16,907 people died due to intentional self-harm with a firearm.
- 11,920 people died due to assault with a firearm.
- 347 died from legal intervention (police, etc.) with a firearm.
- 232 people died from firearms discharge, intent unknown.

In September 2004, the 1994 federal ban on assault weapons came up for renewal. Congress chose not to renew the ban. Under President George W. Bush, new laws have been passed that require gun sellers to destroy background check information 24 hours after the gun purchase is complete.

Characteristics of Assault Weapons That Have Been Banned

If a gun contains two or more of these features, the assault weapons ban declared it illegal for manufacture and possession in the United States.

Rifles:
- Folding/telescoping stock
- Protruding pistol grip
- Bayonet mount
- Threaded muzzle or flash suppressor
- Grenade launcher

Pistols:
- Magazine outside grip
- Threaded muzzle
- Barrel shroud
- Unloaded weight of 50 ounces (1.4 kg) or more
- Semi-automatic version of a fully automatic weapon

Shotguns:
- Folding/telescoping stock
- Protruding pistol grip
- Detachable magazine capacity
- Fixed magazine capacity greater than 5 rounds

MANUFACTURERS AND GUN SAFETY

Guns are the only product whose manufacture is not regulated by the Consumer Product Safety Commission, even though guns are designed to be a lethal product. Legislation to regulate the manufacture of guns has been

proposed in the past, but it has been
ultimately turned down.

It has been suggested that gun
manufacturers could voluntarily add
safety features to their products.
However, gun manufacturers prefer
to keep their costs low, and so they
do not add these safety features.
Safety measures proposed include
childproofing and personalizing
mechanisms that make it hard for unintended users to
fire a gun, whether on purpose or by accident. They
also include load indicators, which show if a gun is still
loaded, and magazine disconnect safeties, which
prevent a gun from firing as it is being loaded or
unloaded.

It is possible that these measures could prevent
accidental shootings. However, gun manufacturers
claim that it is not their responsibility to make guns
safe. That responsibility, they say, is up to gun owners
and users.

"If you're going to give people an almost unlimited freedom to purchase guns, then our freedom, people who want open doors, open access, is going to be infringed."[1]

—Josh Horowitz, Executive Director of the Coalition to Stop Gun Violence.

Lawsuits

Crime victims and families of people killed with
guns have sued gun manufacturers for a variety of

A Ban on Guns

In Washington, D.C., a recent law banned the possession of all guns. A federal court then found that the ban violated the Second Amendment right to bear arms. The decision may next be reviewed at the Supreme Court level.

damages. They sought to prove that gun manufacturers are knowingly being negligent when they create and advertise products such as rapid-fire assault weapons and cop-killer bullets. They have also sued over lax distribution practices that lead to theft and illegal gun sales, and false advertising, for leading people to believe that guns prevent crime. They hoped the lawsuits would influence gun manufacturers to introduce safety devices to their guns.

In July 2005, the Senate passed a bill that made it illegal for crime victims to sue gun manufacturers. The bill passed with a large majority.

GUNS AND TECHNOLOGY

Senator Edward Kennedy of Massachusetts and Representative Xavier Becerra of California have introduced a new piece of legislation that would require "microstamping" for guns manufactured after 2009. Microstamping is a procedure that marks bullet casings with serial numbers that could trace a bullet to the gun that fired it. Microstamping would help law enforcement officials track ammunition back to the gun.

Todd Lizotte holds a cartridge case fired from a handgun marked with microstamping technology he developed.

There are other technology measures that could be applied to guns in the future. One such development would be personalized guns, which would recognize and fire only for their owner. It is hoped that this technology could cut down on accidental shootings and reduce gun theft, as a stolen gun would be harder to operate. It would also make it easier for law enforcement to identify shooters.

Gun Control and Politics

Gun control supporters have grown increasingly concerned about politicians' lack of interest in gun control policies in recent years. The gun control movement was at full power in the early 1990s when the Brady Law and the assault weapons ban were passed. Since then, political will to enact gun control laws has declined. Gun control was a major campaign issue in 1988 and 1992, but politicians have since stopped calling attention to their positions on gun control.

Politicians in favor of gun control laws may have stopped speaking out because they fear it will hurt them politically. However, gun control supporters say that poll data shows the majority of Americans support stricter gun control policies.

Ballistic Fingerprinting

Each time a gun is used, it leaves a mark on the bullets it fires. The same gun always leaves the same mark, and no two guns have the same mark, even if they are the same kind of gun. These marks are called ballistic fingerprints, and they are used in crime investigations. Law enforcement agencies would like ballistic fingerprint records to be kept for all guns that are sold, so that when guns are used in crimes they are easier to trace. A few states, like New York and Massachusetts, voluntarily store ballistic fingerprint data.

House Democratic leader Les Miller, left, and Representative Tony Hill take part in a news conference highlighting the stalled status of gun safety legislation on April 13, 2000, in Tallahassee, Florida.

GUN CONTROL OPPOSITION AND POLITICS

Gun control opponents believe that the apparent lack of interest in gun control legislation reflects public opinion swaying toward their point of view. The NRA's lobbying efforts succeeded in getting the assault weapons ban and Brady Law background checks to expire when they came up for renewal.

Gun control was something of an issue in the 2000 election, and some people believe that it was a deciding factor in the outcome of the very close presidential vote. Presidential candidate Al Gore was vocal in his opinions with regard to gun control laws following the Columbine High School massacre in 1999. Because a large portion of the U.S. population is opposed to gun control, it is likely that this cost him votes in the election.

Vice President Al Gore gestures toward various assault weapons during a news conference at the Treasury Department in Washington, D.C.

Senator Dianne Feinstein holds an AK-47 automatic rifle during a news conference in Washington, D.C., on March 9, 1999.

GUN CONTROL TODAY

*I*t is amazing how much has changed about guns and gun use since the United States was founded. The guns themselves, people's understanding of the Second Amendment, and the frequency of violent crime have all changed. The future

of guns and gun control remains to
be seen.

CHANGES IN GUNS

The guns available to people
during the American Revolution
were single-shot muskets, rifled
firearms (both long guns and
pistols), and "fowling pieces" (which
were early shotguns). Muzzle-loaded
weapons were fired slowly. It took
time to load the gunpowder, then
insert the bullet, and then a "wad"
(which was a piece of oiled cloth or hide). After
this, the pan was primed and the weapon was fired.

Gun-related Deaths

According to 1966 statis-
tics, approximately 17,000
Americans were killed by
guns annually. Today, the
rate is more than 30,000
gun-related deaths per
year.

Like most everything else in American life, guns
have gotten faster. They have evolved into high-
powered, efficient machines. Guns are more
accurate and deadlier than they have ever been.
The country has seen bullets that explode, bullets
that pierce armor, plastic guns, tiny handguns, high
powered rifles, machine guns that fire hundreds of
bullets per minute, and sniper rifles that shoot from
great distances.

SECOND AMENDMENT TODAY

Something that has not changed about this debate is the text of the Second Amendment. What has changed is the way people interpret that important text. It is just one short sentence, but it has prompted centuries of thought, discussion, disagreement, and compromise. Many books have been written about the Second Amendment and the right to bear arms, and each one has a slightly different take on the issue.

It is exciting, and very American, to be able to debate the gun control issue so heatedly. There are places in the world where citizens cannot speak out about their opinions on controversial issues, and this kind of dialogue is what makes the United States a functioning democracy. Even when Americans stand in such profound opposition to each other, they remain grateful for the opportunity to participate in lawmaking and to contribute to the shaping of their society for years to come.

Gallup Poll on the Second Amendment

A 2003 Gallup NCC poll found that of the 68 percent of respondents who believed that the Second Amendment protects the right to bear arms, 82 percent still believe that the government can regulate firearm ownership to some extent. Only 12 percent believe that the Second Amendment prevents the government from restricting ownership of firearms.

Miss Illinois Michelle LaGroue speaks about handgun violence during a public rally sponsored by the Illinois Council Against Handgun Violence on October 20, 2004, in Chicago, Illinois.

THE DEBATE DIES DOWN?

In January 2007, the number of people who supported stricter gun laws was at 49 percent, less than a majority for the first time since at least 1990. Researchers believe the decline in interest in gun control is related to the decline in violent crime over the same period of time. Though people still feel strongly about gun control on both sides of the issue, during the last few years it has been on the back burner of U.S. politics.

When gun-related incidents arise, the debate is stirred up anew. Gun control supporters lament the presence of guns in society and push for stricter laws that make it harder to get guns. They believe that strong laws will help keep guns from falling into the wrong hands. At the same time, gun control opponents lament the lack of regulations that permit law-abiding citizens to carry concealed weapons. They believe that the death toll from such tragic shooting incidents could be limited by the presence of good citizens with guns.

New Gun Legislation

Two new gun control bills have been introduced to Congess in 2007 by New York Congresswoman Carolyn McCarthy. While these bills have not passed into law, they are currently up for debate.

The Assault Weapons Ban and Law Enforcement Protection Act of 2007: This law would reinstate the 1994 law banning assault weapons. The 1994 law expired in 2004. The 2007 law would expand on the 1994 list of guns that would be banned. This law also bans "detachable magazines." These are devices that hold a large number of bullets and feed them into guns.

The NICS Improvement Act: In response to the Virginia Tech shootings, this bill was introduced to Congress in 2007. It would improve the National Instant Criminal Background Check System. This bill would help stop mentally ill and barred individuals from purchasing guns.

DECISIONS FOR THE FUTURE

The gun laws that exist are constantly under scrutiny by government, lawmakers, law enforcement, lobbyists, gun owners, crime victims, and average citizens. What will the nation ultimately decide is right for the United States and guns?

Congress will soon consider whether to pass new laws regarding gun-show background checks. New legislation is also being explored that would strengthen the NICS background check system to include more detailed information about gun buyers. It would also reinstitute and expand the assault weapons ban. The Child Proof Guns Act will be considered in the House of Representatives shortly as well.

Individual states have taken action either for or against gun control. In Texas, the concealed carry weapons law has been supported by new legislation that allows expanded rights for individuals to use lethal

Background Checks

According to research in a 2002 report by the Americans for Gun Safety Foundation, just one in every 75,000 people who tried to buy a gun was denied by the background check system due to mental health reasons. The same report indicated that as many as 2.6 million previously institutionalized people may be excluded from the background check system. Gun control supporters worry that within this population there may be some individuals who could be dangerous to themselves or others if allowed to purchase guns. They would like to see background check systems kept more accurately updated in all states.

"Certainly one of the chief guarantees of freedom under any government, no matter how popular and respected, is the right of the citizen to keep and bear arms. This is not to say that firearms should not be very carefully used and that definite rules of precaution should not be taught and enforced. But the right of the citizen to bear arms is just one more safeguard against a tyranny which now appears remote in America, but which historically has proved to be always possible."[1]

—Hubert H. Humphrey, former vice president, 1960

force in self-defense. Several other states have or are considering similar laws.

There may not be a clear right or wrong about the issue of gun control, but the debate is certainly not over. Americans continue to grapple with the text of the Second Amendment, their changing society, and the opinions of each citizen.

*A man chooses a gun at the Gun Gallery in
Glendale, California, on April 18, 2007.*

TIMELINE

1788

The United States Constitution takes effect on June 21.

1791

The Bill of Rights becomes part of the Constitution on December 15.

1792

The Uniform Militia Act of 1792 defines militia members as "all free able-bodied white male citizens" ages 18 to 45.

1918

The United States enters World War I on April 23.

1919

The Eighteenth Amendment takes effect on January 16 and prohibits the sale, production, and transportation of alcohol.

1934

The National Firearms Act of 1934 is enacted on June 26 in response to the rise of gangsters and violent crime.

1861	**1868**	**1871**
South Carolina's militia fires on Union soldiers at Fort Sumter on April 14, starting the Civil War.	The Fourteenth Amendment takes effect on July 9.	The National Rifle Association is founded on November 17.

1938	**1941**	**1963**
The Federal Firearms Act of 1938 is enacted on June 30.	The United States declares war on Japan and enters World War II on December 8.	President John F. Kennedy is assassinated on November 22.

TIMELINE

1968	1968	1968
The Reverend Dr. Martin Luther King, Jr. is assassinated on April 4.	Presidential Candidate Robert F. Kennedy is assassinated on June 5.	The Gun Control Act of 1968 is enacted on October 22.

1989	1990	November 30, 1993
The schoolyard shooting in Stockton, California, occurs on January 17.	The Crime Control Act of 1990 passes on November 29. It includes the Gun Free School Zones Act.	The Brady Handgun Violence Prevention Act is enacted on November 30.

1981

President Ronald Reagan is shot on March 30. James Brady is wounded.

1986

The Firearms Owners' Protection Act of 1986 is enacted on May 19.

1988

The Undetectable Firearms Act of 1988 is enacted on November 10.

1994

The Violent Crime Control and Law Enforcement Act of 1994 is enacted on September 14.

2005

The Senate passes a bill in July that makes it illegal for crime victims to sue gun manufacturers.

2007

The Virginia Tech shooting occurs on April 16 and 30 students are killed.

ESSENTIAL FACTS

AT ISSUE

Opposed

❖ The Second Amendment allows for civilians to own guns.

❖ Widespread gun ownership would decrease gun-related death.

❖ Background checks do not work.

❖ Gun control discriminates against African Americans.

❖ Concealed weapons offer people protection.

❖ Guns can be purchased illegally by criminals.

❖ It is important to teach young people to respect guns.

In Favor

❖ The Second Amendment restricts guns to militia members only.

❖ Getting guns is too easy.

❖ Concealed weapons are a danger to public safety.

❖ Guns in the home should be stored more safely.

❖ Gun ownership correlates to increased gun-related deaths.

❖ Background checks need improvement.

❖ Guns should not be in the hands of young people.

CRITICAL DATES

December 15, 1791
The Bill of Rights became part of the Constitution.

November 17, 1871
The National Rifle Association is founded.

June 26, 1934
The National Firearms Act of 1934 was enacted.

October 22, 1968
The Gun Control Act of 1968 was enacted.

March 30, 1981
James Brady was wounded during an assassination attempt on Ronald Reagan.

November 29, 1990
The Crime Control Act of 1990 passed.

November 30, 1993
The Brady Handgun Violence Prevention Act was enacted.

September 14, 1994
The Violent Crime Control and Law Enforcement Act of 1994 was enacted.

QUOTES

"Certainly one of the chief guarantees of freedom under any government, no matter how popular and respected, is the right of the citizen to keep and bear arms. This is not to say that firearms should not be very carefully used and that definite rules of precaution should not be taught and enforced. But the right of the citizen to bear arms is just one more safeguard against a tyranny which now appears remote in America, but which historically has proved to be always possible." —*Hubert H. Humphrey, former vice president, 1960*

"Show me the man who does not want his gun registered and I will show you a man who should not have a gun."—*Homer Cummings, former U.S. attorney general, 1937*

ADDITIONAL RESOURCES

SELECT BIBLIOGRAPHY

Carter, Gregg Lee. *The Gun Control Movement*. New York: Twayne Publishers, 1997.

Cornell, Saul. *A Well-Regulated Militia: The Founding Fathers and the Origins of Gun Control in America*. Oxford: Oxford University Press, 2006.

Foner, Eric. *The Story of American Freedom*. New York: W.W. Norton & Company, 1998.

Levy, Leonard. *Origins of the Bill of Rights.* New Haven, CT: Yale Nota Bene, 1999.

Spitzer, Robert J. *The Politics of Gun Control*. Chatham, NJ: Chatham House Publishers, 1995.

FURTHER READING

Aitkens, Maggie. *Should We Have Gun Control?* Minneapolis: Lerner Publications, 1992.

Egendorf, Laura, ed. *How Can Gun Violence Be Reduced?* San Diego: Greenhaven Press, 2002.

Streissguth, Tom. *Gun Control: The Pros and Cons*. Berkeley Heights, NJ: Enslow Publishers, 2001.

Web Links

To learn more about gun control, visit ABDO Publishing Company on the World Wide Web at **www.abdopublishing.com**. Web sites about gun control are featured on our Book Links page. These links are routinely monitored and updated to provide the most current information available.

Places to Visit

National Firearms Museum
11250 Waples Mill Road, Fairfax, VA 22030
703-267-1600
www.nationalfirearmsmuseum.org
The National Firearms Museum houses collections of firearms that illustrate the American history of guns. This museum also houses a library with books about firearms, hunting, law enforcement, museum conservation, and animal behavior.

The Brady Center to Prevent Gun Violence
1225 Eye Street, NW, Suite 1100, Washington, DC 20005
202-289-7319
www.bradycenter.org
This organization works to enact gun laws in the United States and provide education on gun violence and its prevention.

**The Legal Action Project of The Brady Center
to Prevent Gun Violence**
1225 Eye Street, Suite 1100, Washington, DC 20005
202-289-7319
www.gunlawsuits.org
This organization is part of the Brady Center and works in the court system to defend gun control laws and assist victims of gun violence.

GLOSSARY

abolitionist
A person who wanted to end slavery.

amendment
An addition to the Constitution that changes or adds to its meaning.

arms
Another word for weapons.

assault weapon
A semi-automatic gun that is similar to a gun used in the military.

Bill of Rights
The first ten amendments to the United States Constitution.

communism
A political theory that supports state-wide ownership of all property and no private property.

firearm
A weapon from which a shot is fired by a gunpowder reaction.

founding fathers
The United States' first leaders who were colonists who led the Revolutionary War and wrote the Constitution and Bill of Rights.

gangster
A person who is part of a violent criminal gang.

industrialization
A time when advances in technology and the invention of machines made it easier to produce large volumes of goods.

infringe
To violate or try to take away.

lobbying
Organizing people to ask lawmakers to vote a certain way.

militia
A citizen army made up of trained and well-regulated volunteer soldiers.

musket
A muzzle-loaded gun with a long barrel, used in the Revolutionary War.

right
The freedom or permission to take a certain action.

self-defense
The ability to defend oneself through physical force.

tyranny
Leadership or rule by a person or group that is very controlling, that forces a country's citizens to follow certain laws they disagree with.

Source Notes

Chapter 1. The Gun Control Debate

1. Eric Foner. *The Story of American Freedom*. New York: W.W.Norton & Company, 1998. 321.

2. Ibid. 328.

3. Phyllis Schafly. "Gun Control Will Not Reduce Gun Violence." *How Can Gun Violence Be Reduced?* Ed. Laura K. Egendorf. San Diego: Greenhaven Press, 2002. 14.

4. Daniel Webster and Jens Ludwig. "Concealed-Carry Laws Do Not Save Lives." *How Can Gun Violence Be Reduced?* Ed. Laura K. Egendorf. San Diego: Greenhaven Press, 2002. 48.

Chapter 2. The Right to Bear Arms

1. U.S. Constitution, amend. 2. <http://www.archives.gov/national-archives-experience/charters/bill_of_rights_transcript.html>.

2. Phyllis Schafly. "Gun Control Will Not Reduce Gun Violence." *How Can Gun Violence Be Reduced?* Ed. Laura K. Egendorf. San Diego: Greenhaven Press, 2002. 21

3. Saul Cornell. "'The Second Amendment Doesn't Prohibit Gun Regulation - It In Fact Compels It,' According to Professor Saul Cornell." Interview by Scott Vogel. *Buzzflash Web site*. 4 Sept. 2006. <http://www.buzzflash.com/articles/interviews/029>.

Chapter 3. Militias and Shifting Attitudes

1. John F Romano. "State Militias and the United States: Changed Responsibilities for a New Era." *The Air Force Law Review*. Maxwell AFB:2005. Vol. 56. 233-247.

2. Gregg Lee Carter. *The Gun Control Movement*. New York: Twayne Publishers, 1997. 67.

Chapter 4. Guns and Gun Control in U.S. History

1. U.S. Constitution, amend. 1.
<http://www.archives.gov/national-archives-experience/charters/bill_of_rights_transcript.html>.

2. U.S. Constitution, amend. 4.
<http://www.archives.gov/national-archives-experience/charters/bill_of_rights_transcript.html>.

3. U.S. Constitution, amend. 14.
<http://www.archives.gov/national-archives-experience/charters/bill_of_rights_transcript.html>.

4. U.S. Constitution, amend. 18.
<http://www.archives.gov/national-archives-experience/charters/bill_of_rights_transcript.html>.

5. Tom Head, ed. *The Bill of Rights*. San Diego: Greenhaven Press, 2004. 2.

Chapter 5. Key Players in the Gun Control Debate

1. Robert J. Spitzer. *The Politics of Gun Control*. Chatham, NJ: Chatham House, 1995. 63.

2. Ibid.

3. Violence Policy Center. "Private Gun Ownership leads to Higher Rates of Gun Violence." *Gun Control*. Ed. Helen Cothran. Farmington Hills, MI: Greenhaven Press, 2003. 17.

SOURCE NOTES CONTINUED

4. Ed Stoddard. "Texas signs new self-defense by gun law." Reuters. 27 Mar. 2007. <http://www.reuters.com/article/politicsNews/idUSN2721289620070327>.

Chapter 6. Arguments in Favor of Gun Control

1. U.S. Constitution, amend. 2. <http://www.archives.gov/national-archives-experience/charters/bill_of_rights_transcript.html>.

2. Phil W. Johnston. "Gun Safety Standards Should Not Be Mandatory." *Gun Control*. Ed. Helen Cothran. Farmington Hills, MI: Greenhaven Press, 2003. 170.

3. Ibid. 162.

Chapter 7. Arguments Against Gun Control

1. U.S. Constitution, amend. 2. <http://www.archives.gov/national-archives-experience/charters/bill_of_rights_transcript.html>.

2. Robert A. Heinlein. *Beyond This Horizon*. Riverdale, NY: Baen Books, 2001.

3. Gregg Lee Carter. *The Gun Control Movement*. New York: Twayne Publishers, 1997.

4. Robert J. Spitzer. *The Politics of Gun Control*. Chatham, NJ: Chatham House, 1995. 1.

Chapter 8. Minors and Guns

1. Teenage Research Unlimited. June 2003. ICHV Web site. 27 June 2007 <http://www.ichv.org/Statistics.htm>.

2. Jennifer Parker and Teddy Davis. "Culture or Control: Guns Spark Intense Political Debate." ABC News. 17 Apr. 2007. <http://abcnews.go.com/Politics/print?id=95437>.

Chapter 9. Recent Developments in Gun Legislation

1. Jennifer Parker and Teddy Davis. "Culture or Control: Guns Spark Intense Political Debate." ABC News. 17 Apr. 2007. <http://abcnews.go.com/Politics/print?id=95437>.

Chapter 10. Gun Control Today

1. Hubert H. Humphrey. "Know Your Lawmakers." *Guns Magazine*. Feb. 1960. 6.

INDEX

ABOUT THE AUTHOR

Kekla Magoon has a Master of Fine Arts in Writing for Children and Young Adults from Vermont College. Her work includes many different kinds of writing, but she especially enjoys writing historical fiction and non-fiction. When she is not writing books for children, she works with non-profit organizations and helps with fundraising for youth programs.

PHOTO CREDITS

Nick Ut/AP Images, cover, 3; Douglas C. Pizac/AP Images, 6; Ron Edmonds/AP Images, 10, 99 (top); Ric Feld/AP Images, 13, 97 (top); Justin Merriman/Getty Images, 15; NARA, 16, 96 (top); Carolyn Kaster/AP Images, 23; Nancy Palmieri/AP Images, 24; Kathleen Lange/AP Images, 29; Elena Hougton/AP Images, 31, 62; AP Images, 32, 36, 96 (bottom); Alfred Eisenstaedt/Time Life Pictures/Getty Images, 41, 97 (bottom); Jack Manning/New York Times Co./Getty Images, 43; Vince Bucci/AFP/Getty Images, 44; Luke Frazza/AFP/Getty Images, 47, 98 (right); April L. Brown/AP Images, 53; Gene J. Puskar/AP Images, 54; Paul Vernon/AP Images, 57; Adele Starr/AP Images, 61; Lindaanne Donohoe, 67; E.J. Flynn/AP Images, 69; Alan Kim/The Roanoke Times/AP Images, 70, 99 (bottom); Eric Gay/AP Images, 75; Chris Livingston/Getty Images, 77; Dennis Cook/AP Images, 78, 83, 87, 88, 98 (left); Mark Foley/AP Images, 85; Tim Boyle/Getty Images, 91; Gabriel Bouys/AFP/Getty Images, 95